EXPLORE THE WORLD

SOCIAL SCIENCE

The Mail

ZANE WALTERS

TABLE OF CONTENTS

The Mail	2
History of Mail	4
Moving the Mail	8
Stamps	12
Modern Technology and the Mail	16
Glossary/Index	20

PIONEER VALLEY EDUCATIONAL PRESS, INC

THE MAIL

Do you like to get letters and cards in the mail? Many people enjoy receiving mail. People like opening the mailbox and finding a letter, **invitation**, or card inside. Mail is a way to **transport** letters and packages from one person to another.

HISTORY OF MAIL

Long ago, when people first began to write, they wanted to share their written messages with each other. They began to find ways to send mail. The mail was transported from one person to another in all kinds of ways.

Mail was once delivered by pigeons. The pigeons would be taken from their home to another place.

Messages would be attached to the pigeons' legs, and the pigeons would fly back home, where the owners could read the message.

Mail has also been delivered by horses, dogsleds, camels, mules, and even hot air balloons.

Long ago, the person who received a letter paid for it. The cost for the mail depended on how far the mail traveled and how heavy it was. Now it is the person sending the mail who pays for it by buying a stamp.

Benjamin Franklin became one of the first leaders of the postal service. He found ways to make it easier to receive mail.

It took a very long time to deliver the mail. Benjamin Franklin arranged for riders to carry the mail day and night.

He arranged for mail to be delivered to people's homes for a penny.

Letters and packages would travel from post office to post office.

MOVING THE MAIL

People moved farther and farther west. New ways were needed to deliver the mail.

Stagecoaches, known as mail coaches, began to transport mail out West on roads. Fast-moving steamboats transported mail up and down rivers in areas where there were no roads.

People living in the eastern United States would get their mail quickly. But if you lived in the West, you might have had to wait for months to get your mail.

When gold was discovered in California, many people moved to the West. A new mail system was created to keep people in the West connected to the rest of the country. It was called the Pony Express.

The Pony Express had more than 100 stations and 80 riders. The route was very dangerous, but only one mail delivery was lost. The Pony Express ended when a special wire that stretched across the country, called a **telegraph** line, was finished, and messages could be sent electronically.

By the 1880s, trains became a very important way for mail to be transported. The mail traveled on most of the passenger trains that crisscrossed the country.

The fast-moving trains helped people living in far-off places to send their mail in a shorter amount of time.

MORE TO EXPLORE

Sometimes people even **mailed children**! In 1914, a four-year-old girl was "mailed" from her home in Idaho to her grandparents' house about 73 miles away. **Postage** was less expensive than a train ticket!

STAMPS

A stamp is placed on an envelope or package to show a fee has been paid. The postage fee is now paid by the sender, not the person receiving the mail.

The first stamps were hand stamps made of wood or cork that were dipped in ink and pressed on the envelope.

The first **adhesive** stamp was used in Britain in 1840 and could be stuck on an envelope. Other countries around the world soon began to do the same thing.

The first British adhesive stamp featured an image of Queen Victoria.

The first five-cent and ten-cent US stamps were made in 1847.

Stamps have been printed in a lot of different ways since then. There are chocolate-flavored stamps, stamps that look and feel like tiny soccer balls, and stamps with swans made of real crystal.

Stamp collecting has become a popular hobby. People like to collect stamps from different places and times.

MODERN TECHNOLOGY AND THE MAIL

Airplanes, cars, and trucks have made it easier to deliver mail. Mail can now be quickly sent to almost any country in the world.

Post offices send thousands of letters and packages each day. Machines were invented to help sort mail quickly. Today, a letter can reach you at your home from across the country in just a few days, or even overnight!

US post offices deliver over 500 million pieces of mail every day.

There are now many new ways to send mail too. People use email to send messages. People use their phones to text each other messages. Fewer people send written mail.

In the future, packages and letters may be delivered to your doorstep by remote-controlled **drones**!

MORE TO EXPLORE

In one place in the United States, the mail is still **DELIVERED BY A MULE TRAIN.** Each day, 50 horses and mules go down a steep trail to deliver mail to a small Native American reservation at the bottom of a canyon in Arizona.

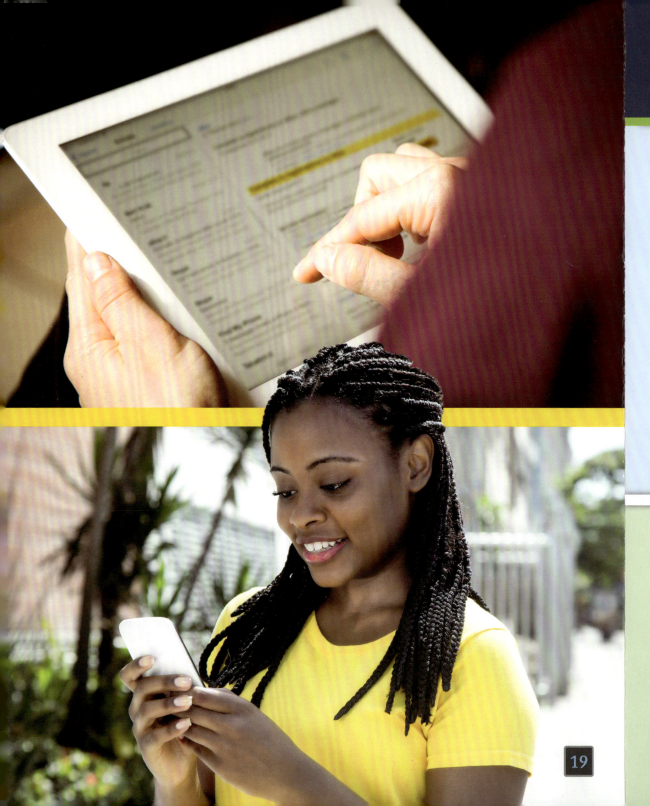

GLOSSARY

adhesive
coated with glue or paste

drones
flying robots that can be remotely controlled

invitation
a message asking someone to go somewhere or do something

postage
the charge for sending a letter or package

stagecoaches
carriages pulled by horses

telegraph
a system for sending messages using wires and electronic machines

transport
to carry or move from one place to another

INDEX

adhesive 13
Benjamin Franklin 7
Britain 13
California 9
camels 5
dogsleds 5
drones 18
email 18
horses 5, 18
hot air balloons 5
invitation 2
mail coaches 8
mailbox 2
messages 4-5, 18
mules 5, 18
pigeons 5
Pony Express 9-10
postage 11-12
post office 7, 16-17
riders 7, 10
routes 8, 10
stagecoaches 8
stamp 6, 12-15
stations 10
steamboats 8
telegraph 10
text 18
trains 11
transport 2, 4, 8, 11
United States 9, 18